ARCHETYPAL POSTURES

In the Process of Creativity

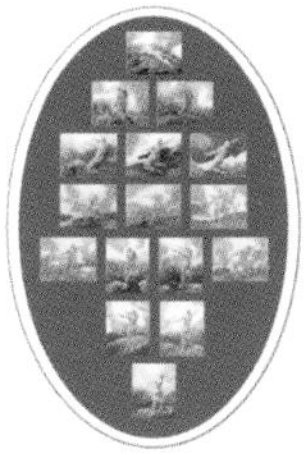

Ian Hopton

La Fontbelle Press

First published in 2005 by:
La Fontbelle Press
10 Greenham Rd. London N10 1LP

A catalogue record for this publication is available from the British Library

ISBN 0-9551078-0-6

Printed by BAS Printers, Salisbury, UK

CONTENTS

FOREWORD

This booklet is a record of one of the typical ceremonies that took place during the life drawing classes conducted by the visionary painter Cecil Collins in the 1970s and 1980s. It also includes a description of his unique teaching methods.

Cecil was a deeply spiritual man, a brilliant teacher who knew how to develop a student's talent through the practice of life drawing. He had a profound understanding of the nature of art and its relationship to practical philosophy. He understood the elements of creativity, perhaps the most elusive of which is spontaneity.

His methods were exacting and disciplined, even discomfiting, but they brought out the latent creative powers in each student.

He recognised the value of ceremony, one of which was the demonstration of creativity through a series of archetypal postures that were enacted by all the students and the model.

The ceremony was conducted with solemnity and reverence, and was indeed deeply moving and memorable. The text and images that follow are its record.

Direct quotations by Cecil are shown in italics.

The images are digitally enhanced prints derived from a set of original collographs* which I made as an immediate visual response to the ceremony. They are entirely my own work and make no visual reference to any of Cecil Collins' paintings or drawings. The text was compiled many years later when the idea of making a booklet arose, and is derived from memory and notes that I made during the ceremony and over a period of six years attending Cecil's life drawing and life painting classes.

Ian Hopton, July 2005

* Collograph is a technique, traditionally using gesso, glue and sand, whereby a relief image may be created above the surface of a plate (as opposed to an etching, where the image is created below the surface). The plate may then be inked up by normal 'intaglio' wiping and prints obtained in the same way as for an etching.

SYMBOLISM of the ARCHETYPES

During the ceremony Cecil made comments on each posture and the following account is the best recollection from memory and notes of what he said.

The process of creativity is from the horizontal to the vertical. The movements represent the unfolding of creation. The feelings generated within the space created by the face and the palms of the hands is crucial.

The first posture, prostrate, represents the state of total submission and surrender prior to any creative act. The first response to the creative urge is to overcome the inertia of passivity and raise the body from the ground to a kneeling position. This act in itself is symbolic of Man's capacity to free himself from the earthbound condition of the animal, subject entirely to the laws of nature. Being aware of his boldness he is nevertheless overcome with humility as expressed in the first kneeling posture with the face down and the palms forward.

In the second kneeling posture the head remains down but the arms are raised forward with palms up, and this expresses a condition of appeal, as though for guidance.

This leads to the third kneeling posture in which the head is raised and the gaze is straight forward. This represents a condition of seeking and enquiry and perhaps symbolises the role of the intellect in the creative process.

The fourth kneeling posture is where the arms are outstretched, the palms still upwards. This is a very open gesture of worship and acknowledgement. In this posture one becomes very aware of the relationship between the face and the palms of the hands and of the lines of energy between.

For the fifth kneeling posture the face is raised upwards with the arms remaining outstretched and this symbolises the condition of joy and rejoicing; the natural outcome of creativity.

The man, further emboldened, takes the next step and adopts the half-kneeling posture which represents the critical moment of decision. It represents a state of transition. It cannot be sustained. The man must commit himself to go forward or relapse. But in the process of creativity he must decide to go forward; there is no turning back.

The first half-kneeling posture is again with head down and palms forward, representing humility, and the four succeeding postures follow the same pattern as for the kneeling position, thus completing eleven postures.

With the twelfth posture the man now rises to his full stature which is the standing position but he repeats the same sequence of five postures beginning with humility then appeal, seeking, worship and finally rejoicing which in this last standing position also represents exultation.

The students remain in each posture for a minute or so in silence and a state of awareness that naturally increases as the ceremony proceeds.

To describe these postures as archetypes is not an exaggeration. Participating within a group in this ceremony enabled one to experience the meaning of symbolism as an existing reality not as some remote intellectual concept lifted from another age or another culture. One became aware of some connection with an ancient knowledge of Man's fundamental condition and perhaps his capacity to re-discover his own divine nature through the creative process.

LIST OF IMAGES

1.

‘From complete disillusionment there can come only two things; final decay and death, or the birth of a faith’

Cecil Collins: Vision of the Fool

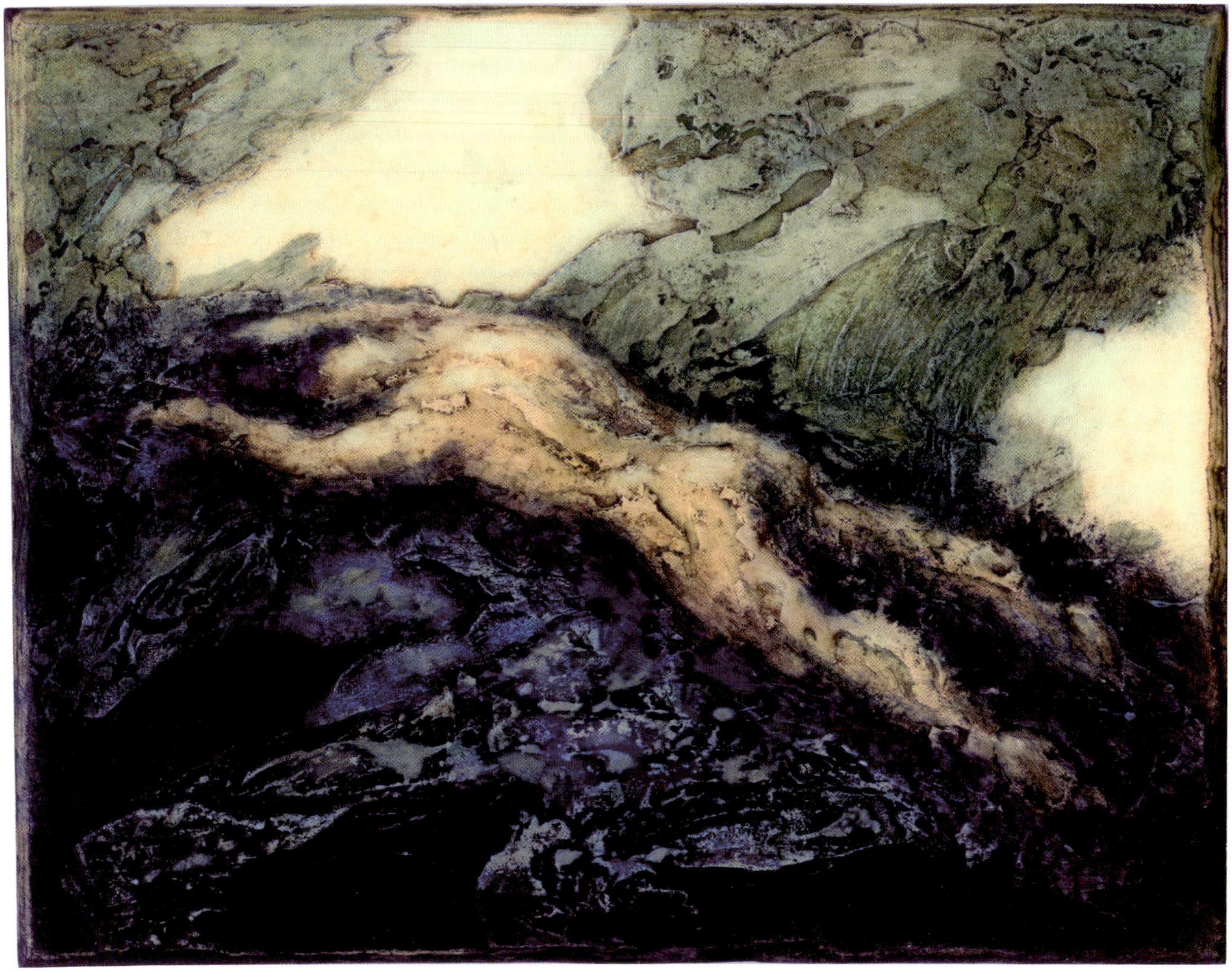

2

'Only real things become myths and legends'

Cecil Collins: The Eternal Presence

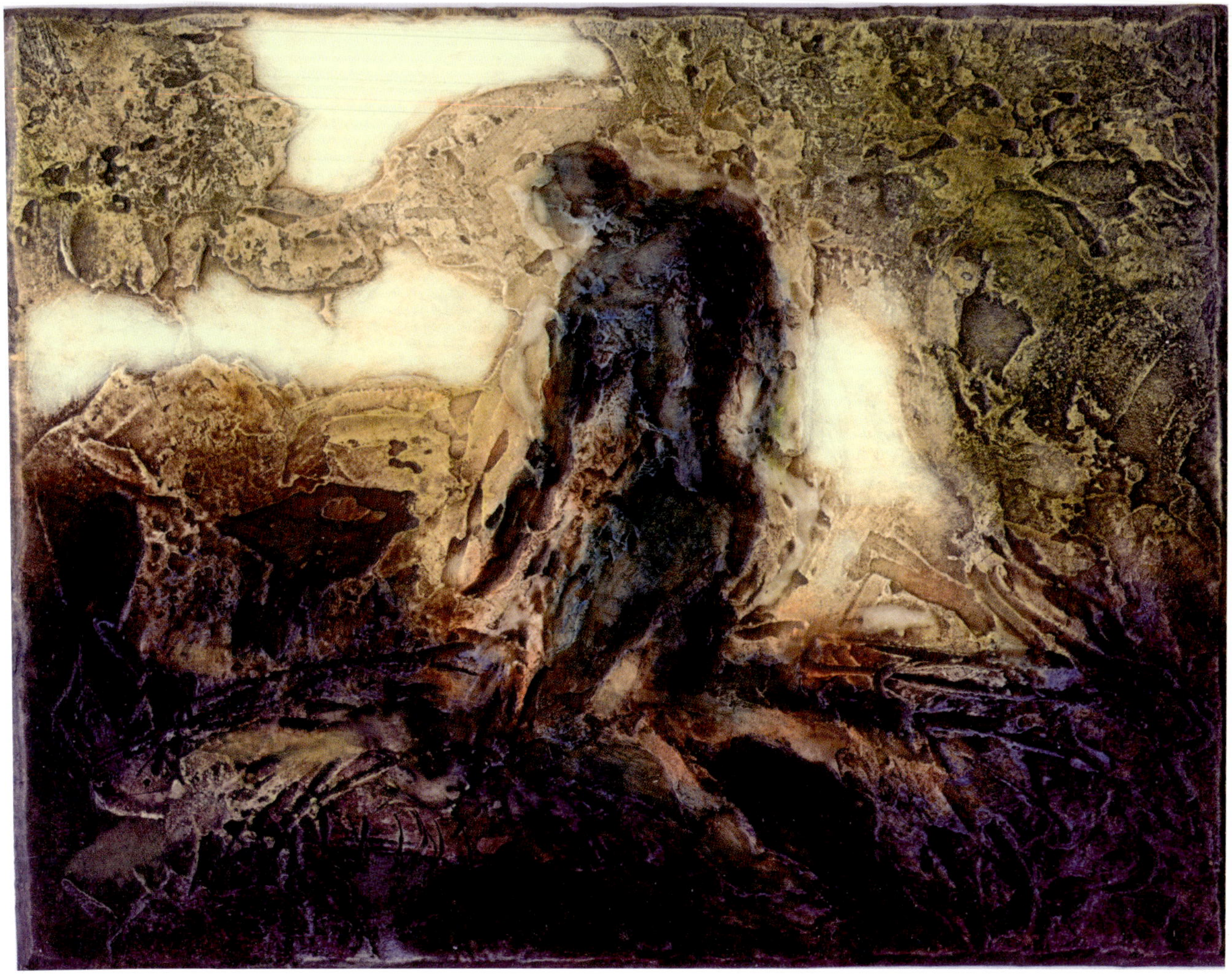

3

'Images arise from the fountain head of human life, the heart, the solar centre, from ancient memories within the blood, and from the polarity and fire of the spirit'

Cecil Collins: Hymn of Life

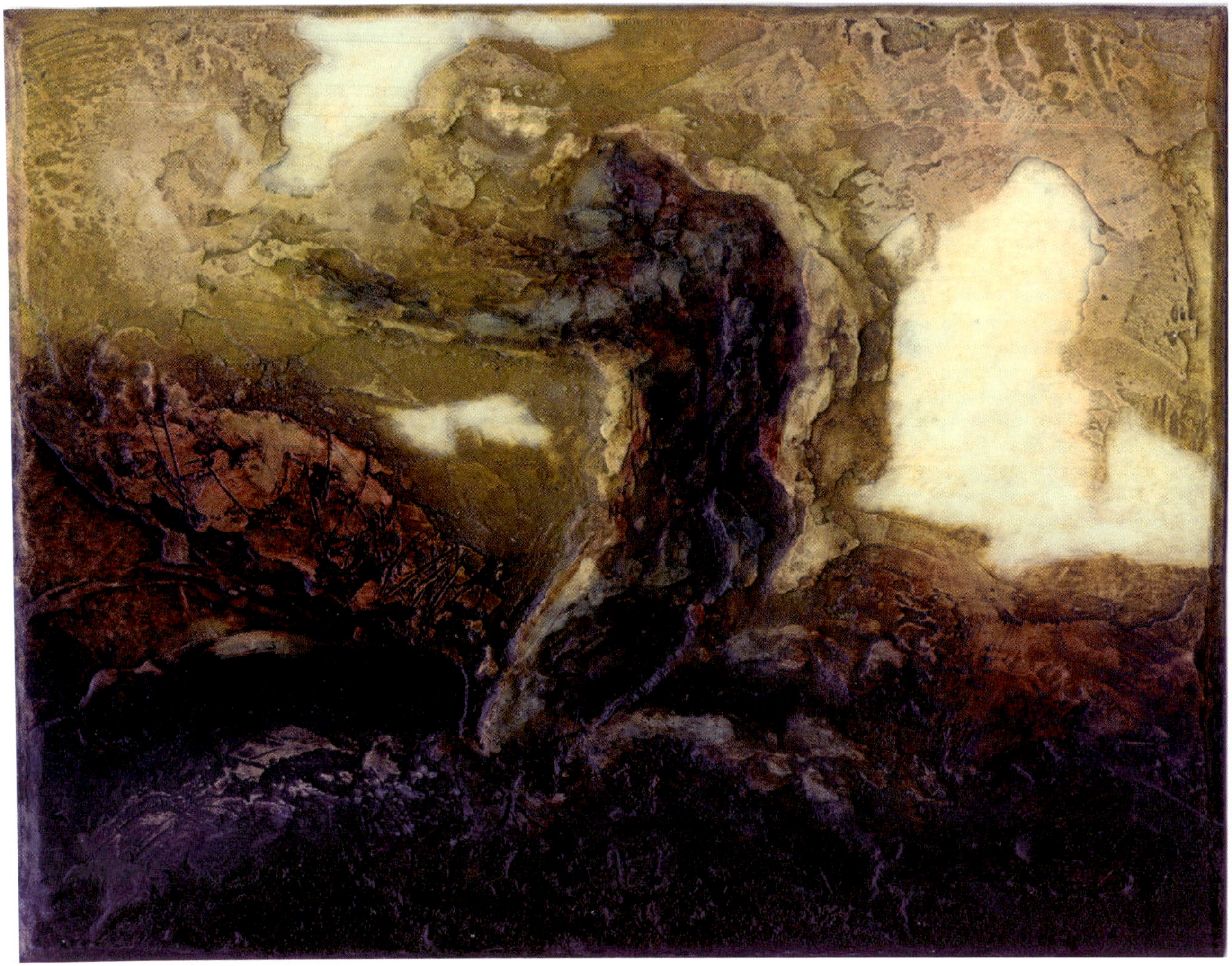

4

'God, the primary reality of the universe, is unknowable and incomprehensible. Symbolism and mythology thus become inevitable'

Cecil Collins: Hymn of Life

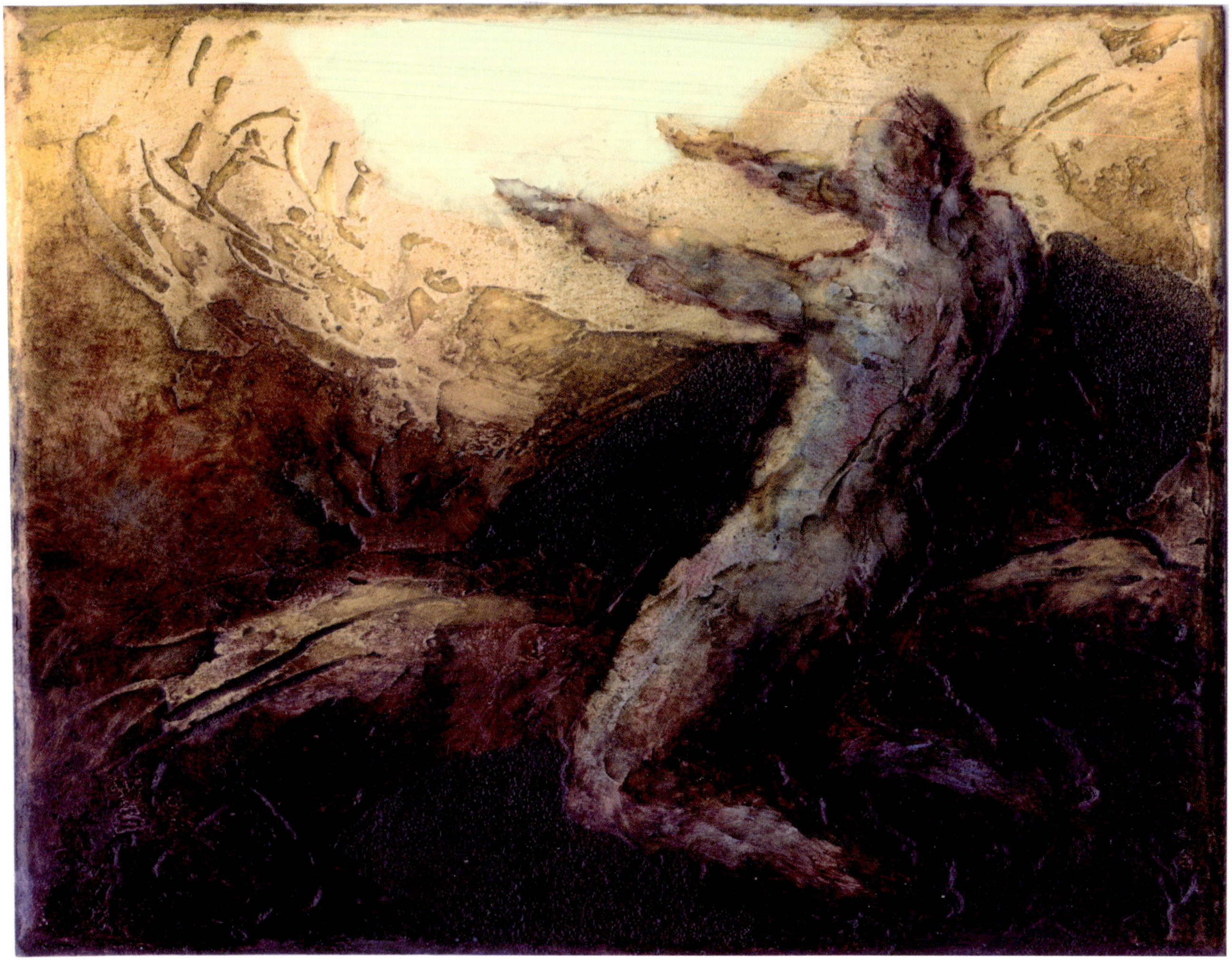

5

'We are alive according to the degree we are in contact with our fundamental nature, our essential self, our essence. This self, this essence, is that within us that knows everything. Therefore in searching for knowledge, for beauty outside, we are wasting our life, for we have within us that which knows all , is all, the Person, the God in us'

Cecil Collins: Hymn of Life

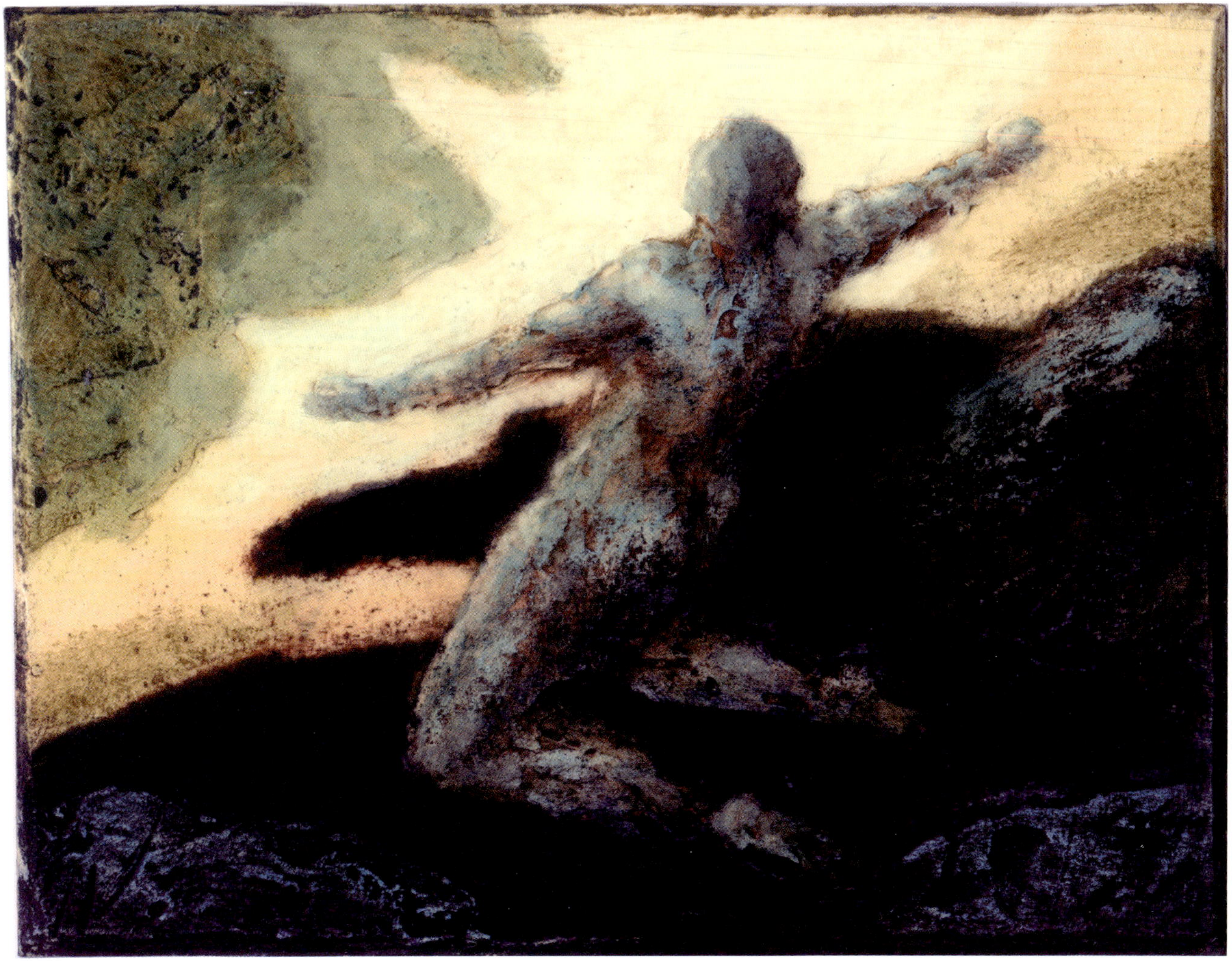

6

'We have to contact the centre of our being because there we have contact with the centre of the universe'

Cecil Collins: Art and Modern Man

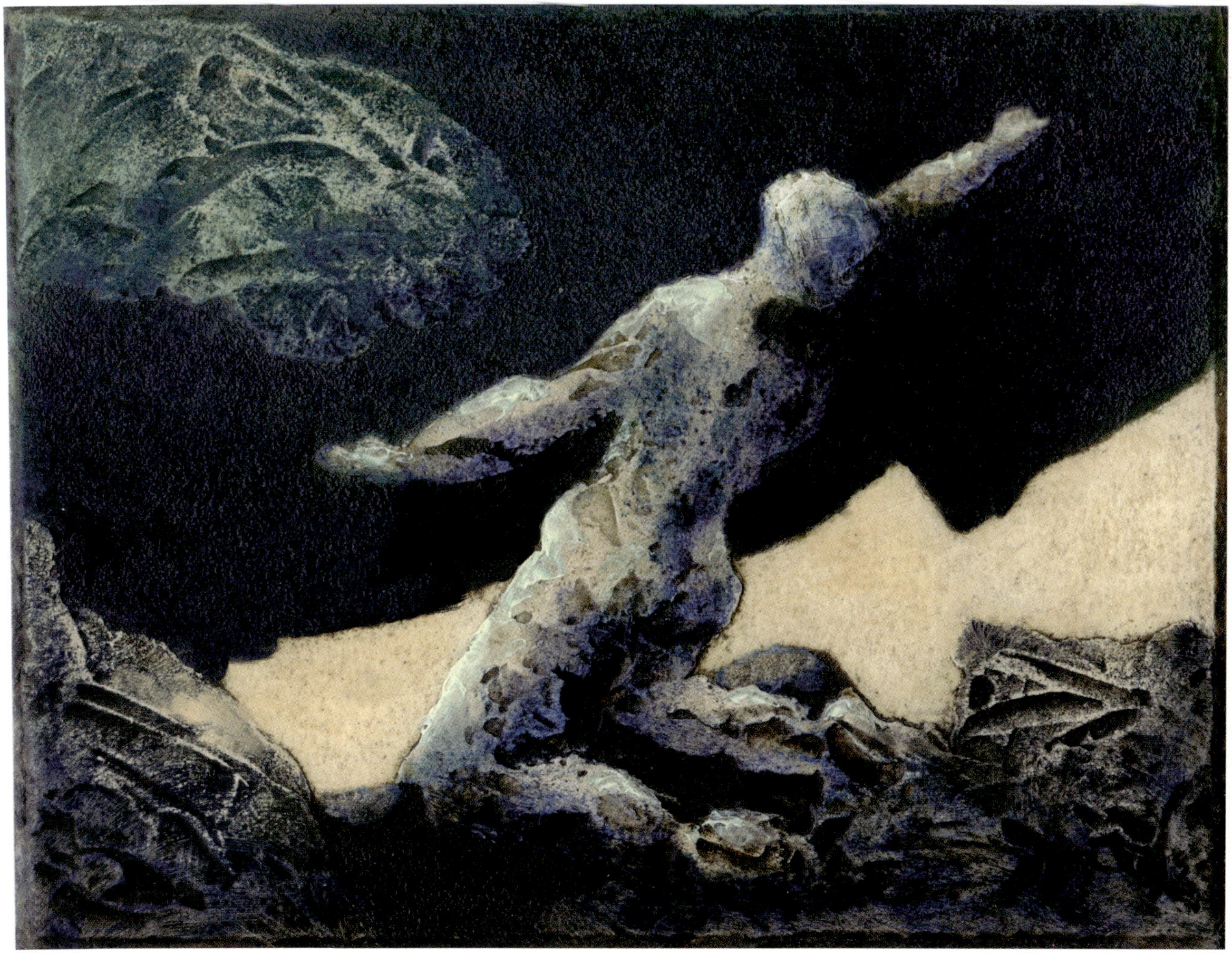

7

'In the moving of the years there is often a quietude when something is trying to be remembered. If only we could believe, would not our sorrow turn upward and remember'

Cecil Collins: *Hymn of Life*

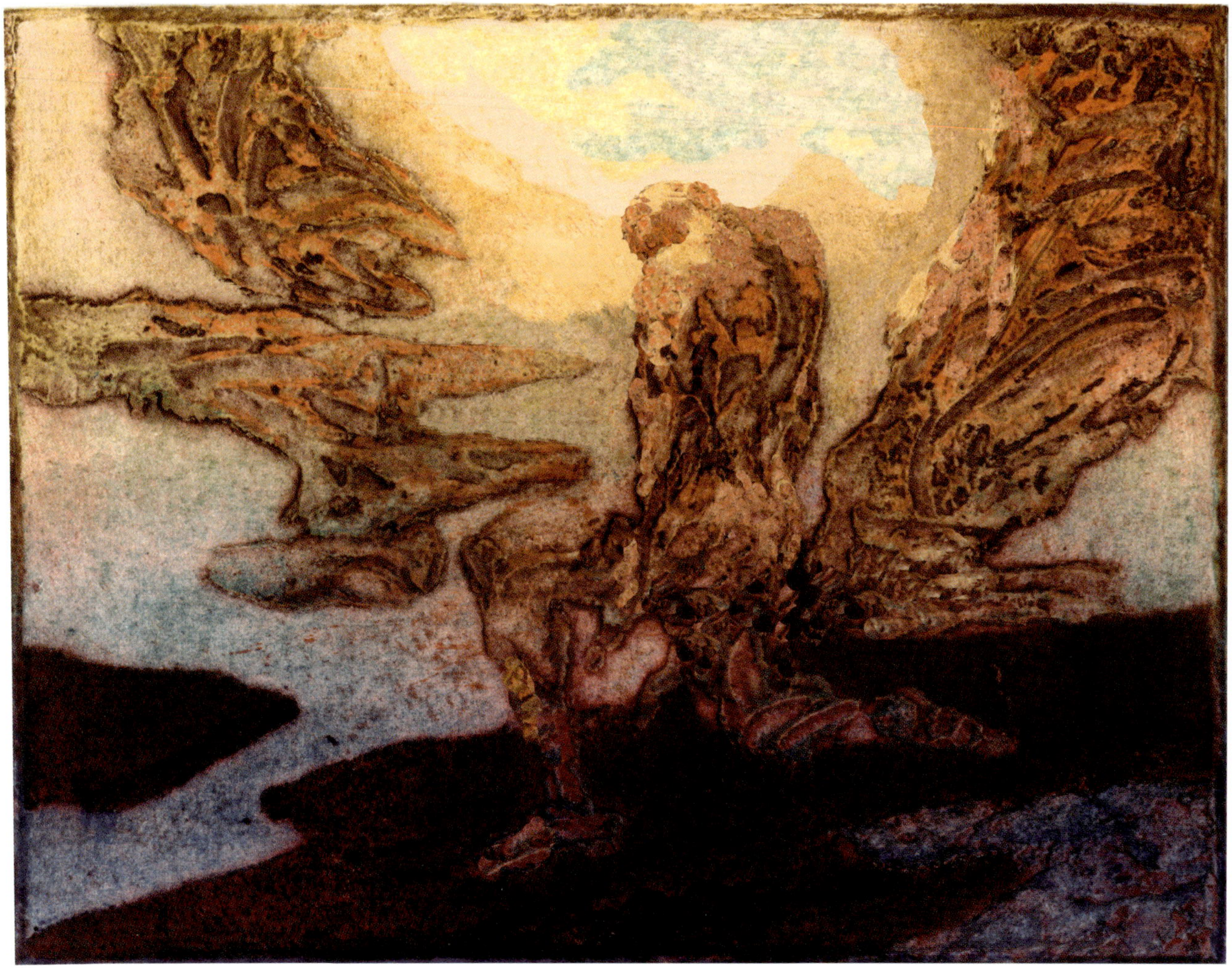

8

'The pilgrimage of life for all beings is through Hell, that is suffering, growth to heaven, which is purification, fruition, happiness and the accomplishment of this existence'

Cecil Collins: Hymn of Life

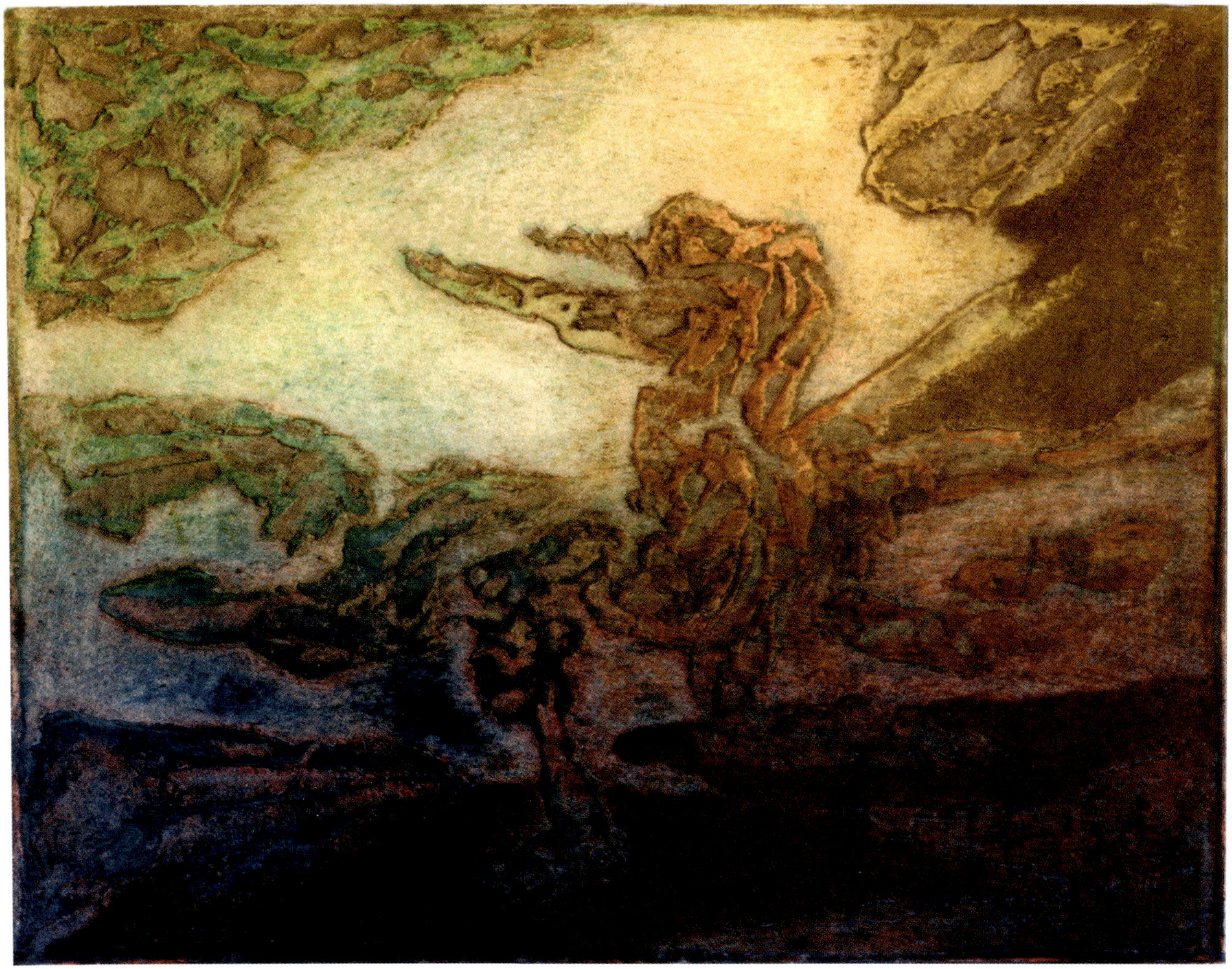

9

'The artist is always concerned with the impossible. He is moved by the impossible, stimulated by the impossible, haunted by the impossible'

Cecil Collins: The Artist in the New Age

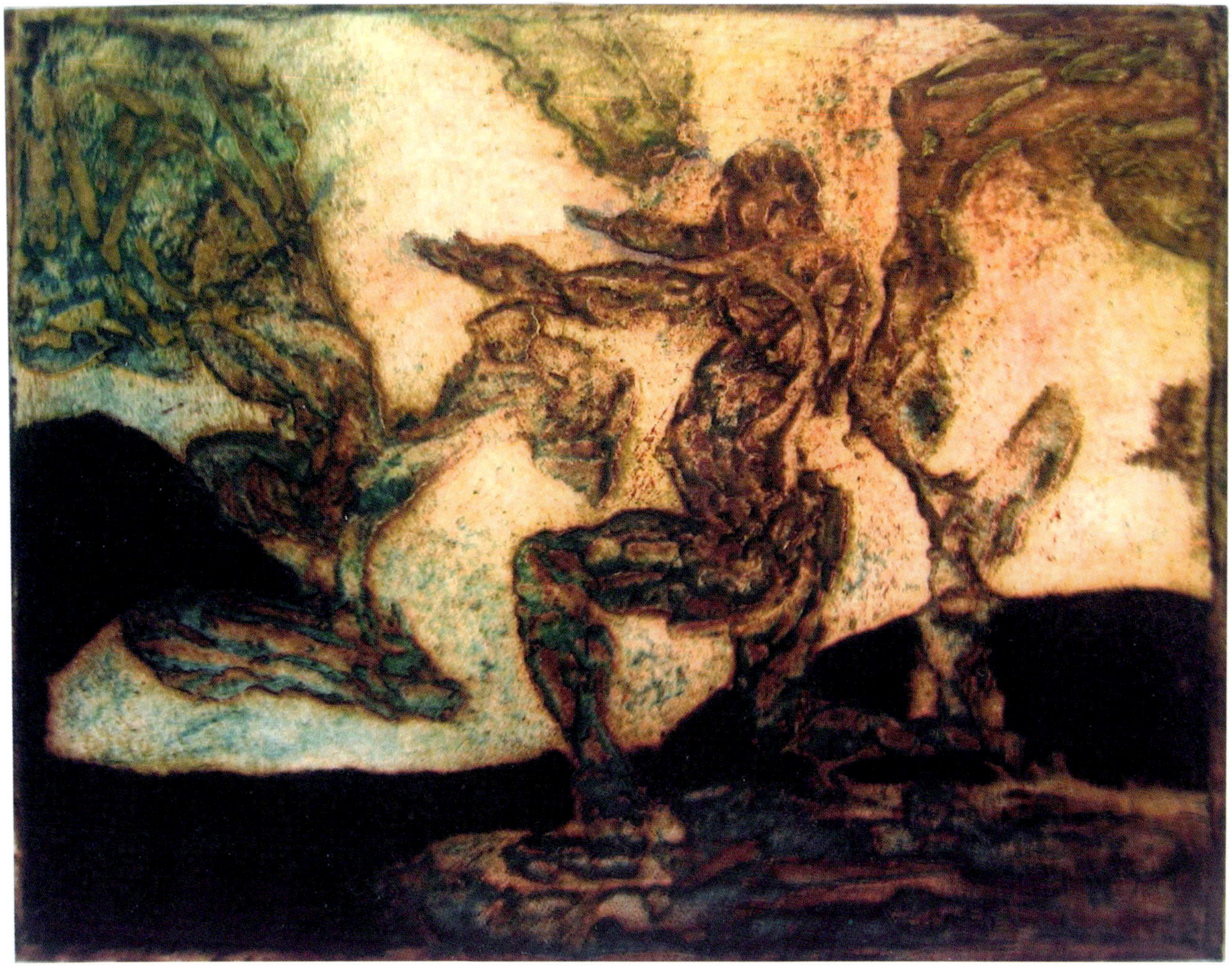

10

'For an artist the greatest happiness is to have failed at doing the perfect, and the greatest misery is never to have attempted it. I believe this is true of all human beings, whether they are creative artists or not. Once the archetype enters the mind you are haunted by a perfection. If you are haunted by a perfection, an ideal, you are unhappy, and the more unhappy you are the more alive you are'

Cecil Collins: The Artist in the New Age

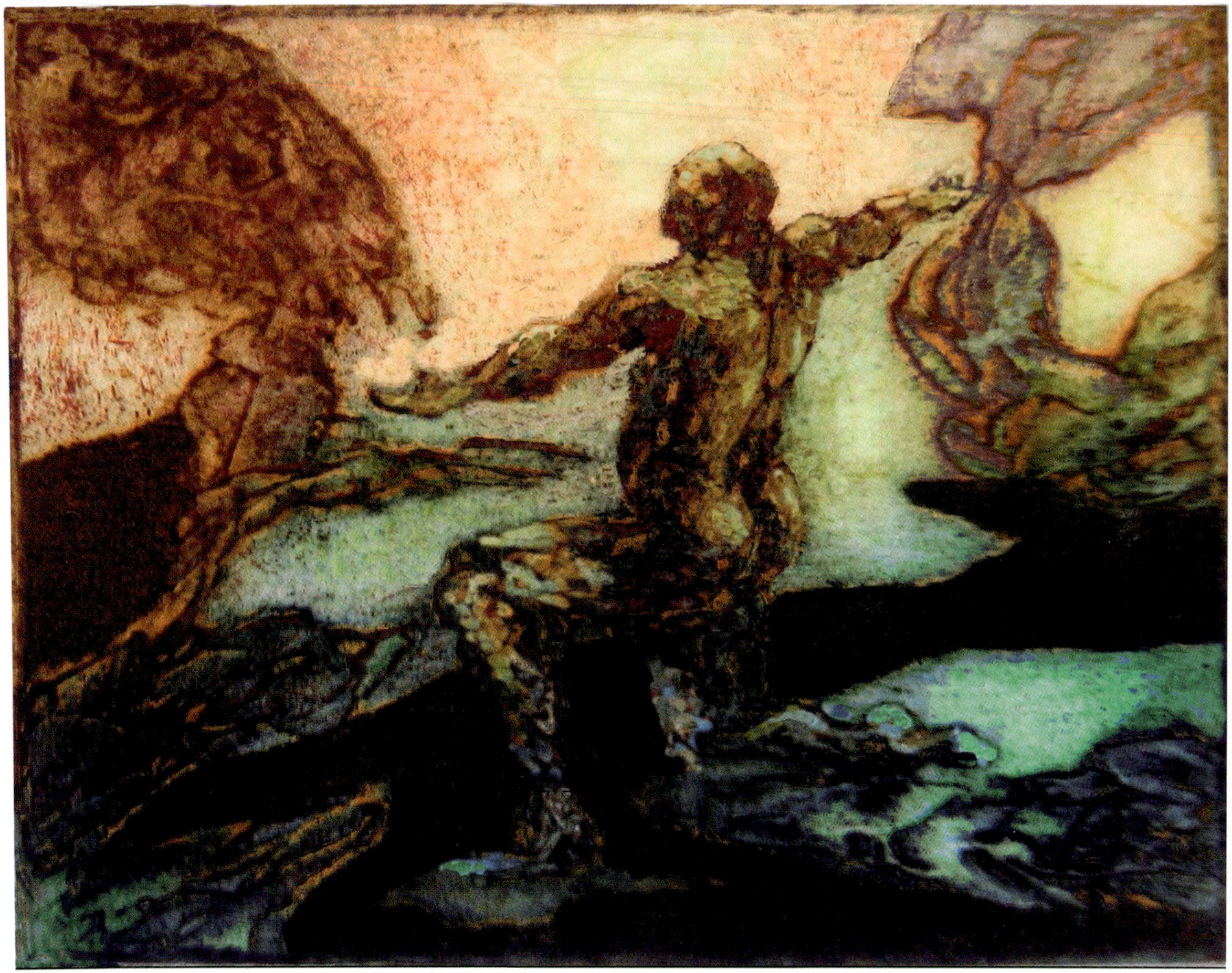

11

'The Saint, the artist, the poet and the Fool are one. They are the eternal virginity of spirit, which in the dark winter of the world continually proclaims the existence of a new life, gives faithful promise of the spring, of an invisible kingdom and the coming of the light'

Cecil Collins: The Vision of the Fool

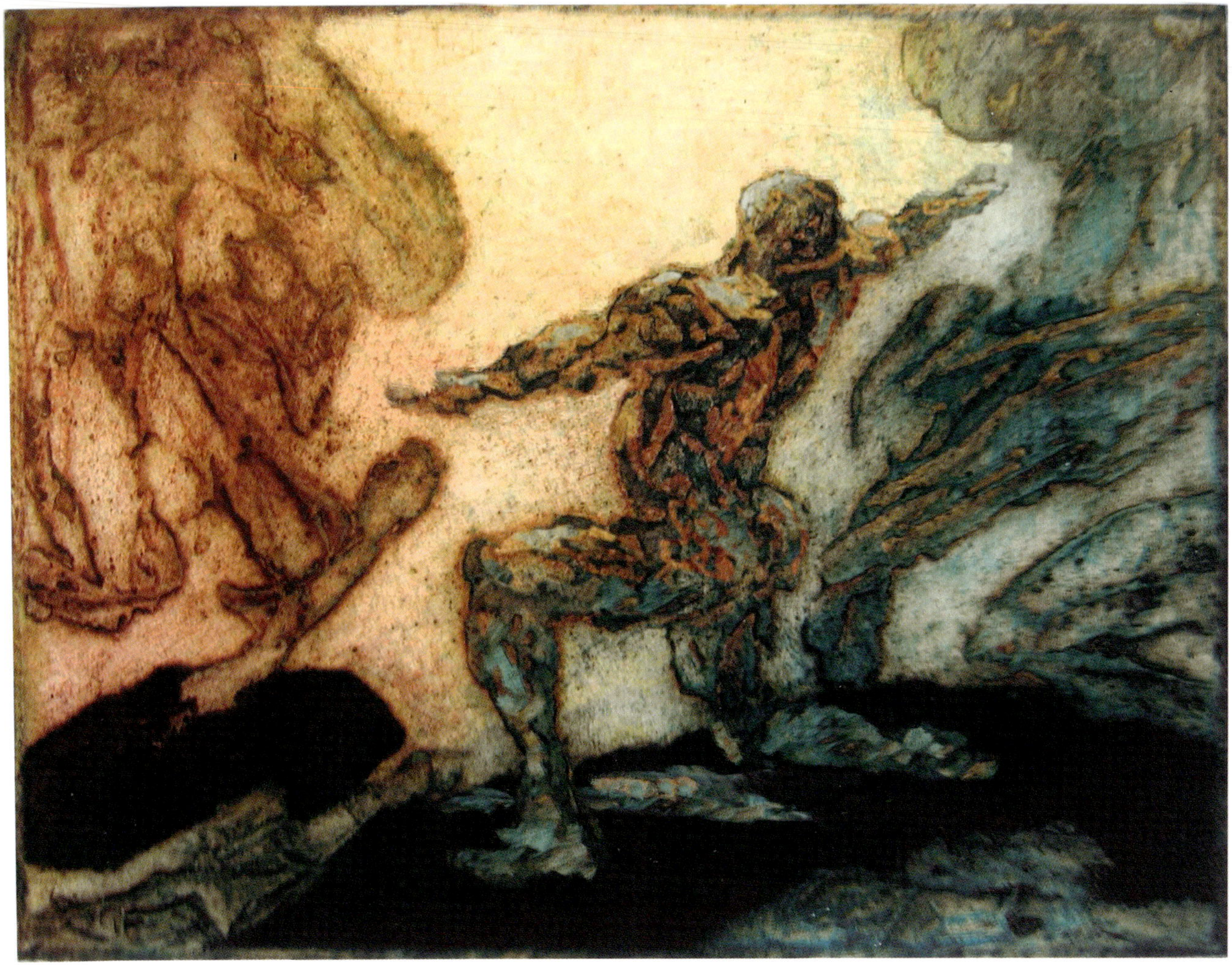

12

'Art is wish fulfilment and recollection. We desire and wish for that beauty we once had. We cannot wish for what we have never known; we cannot paint forms we have never seen'

Cecil Collins: Hymn of Life

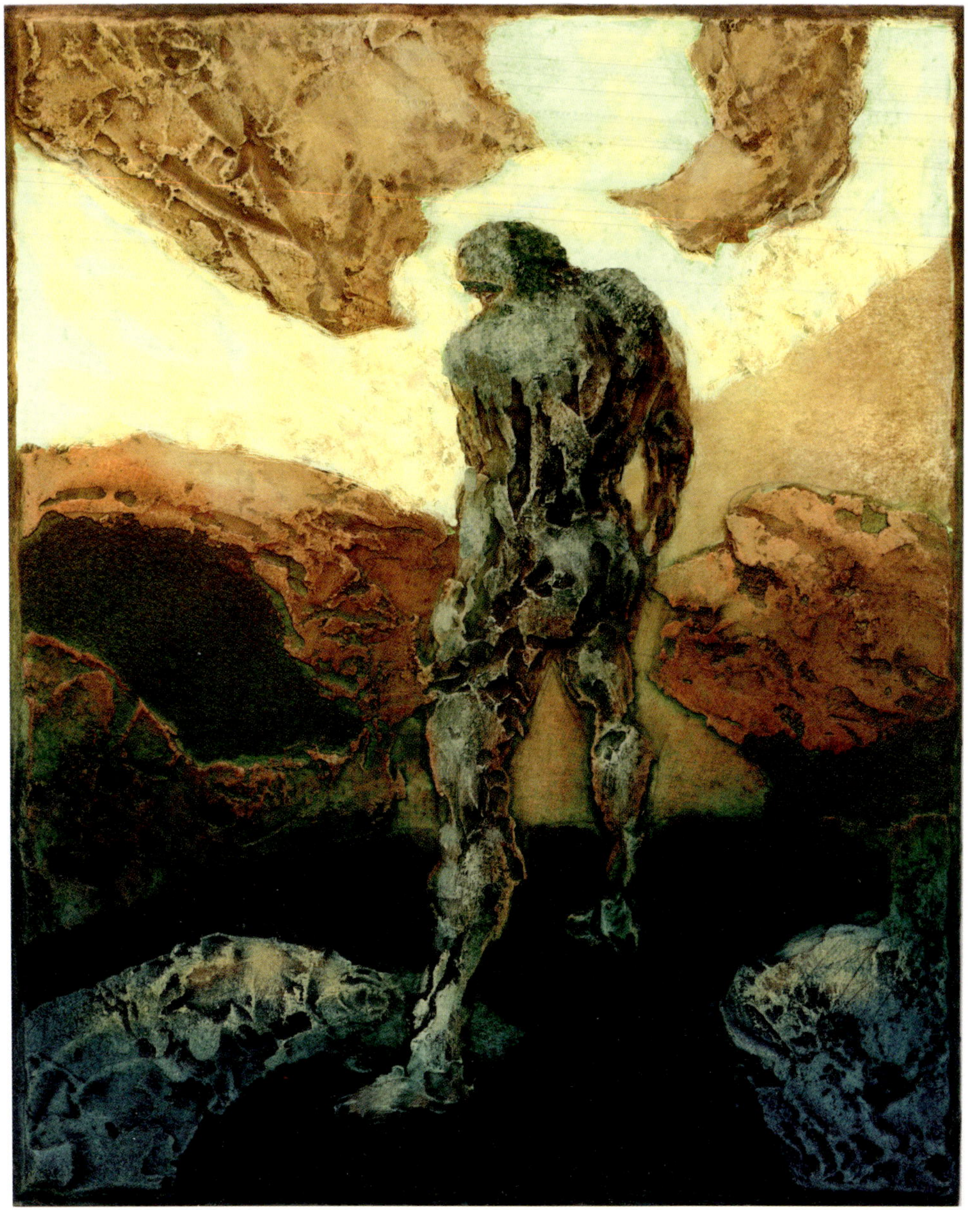

13

'The great energies and vibrations flow down from the centre of the universe into all the worlds, returning again, transforming all the worlds through love, death and transfiguration'

Cecil Collins: Art and Modern Man

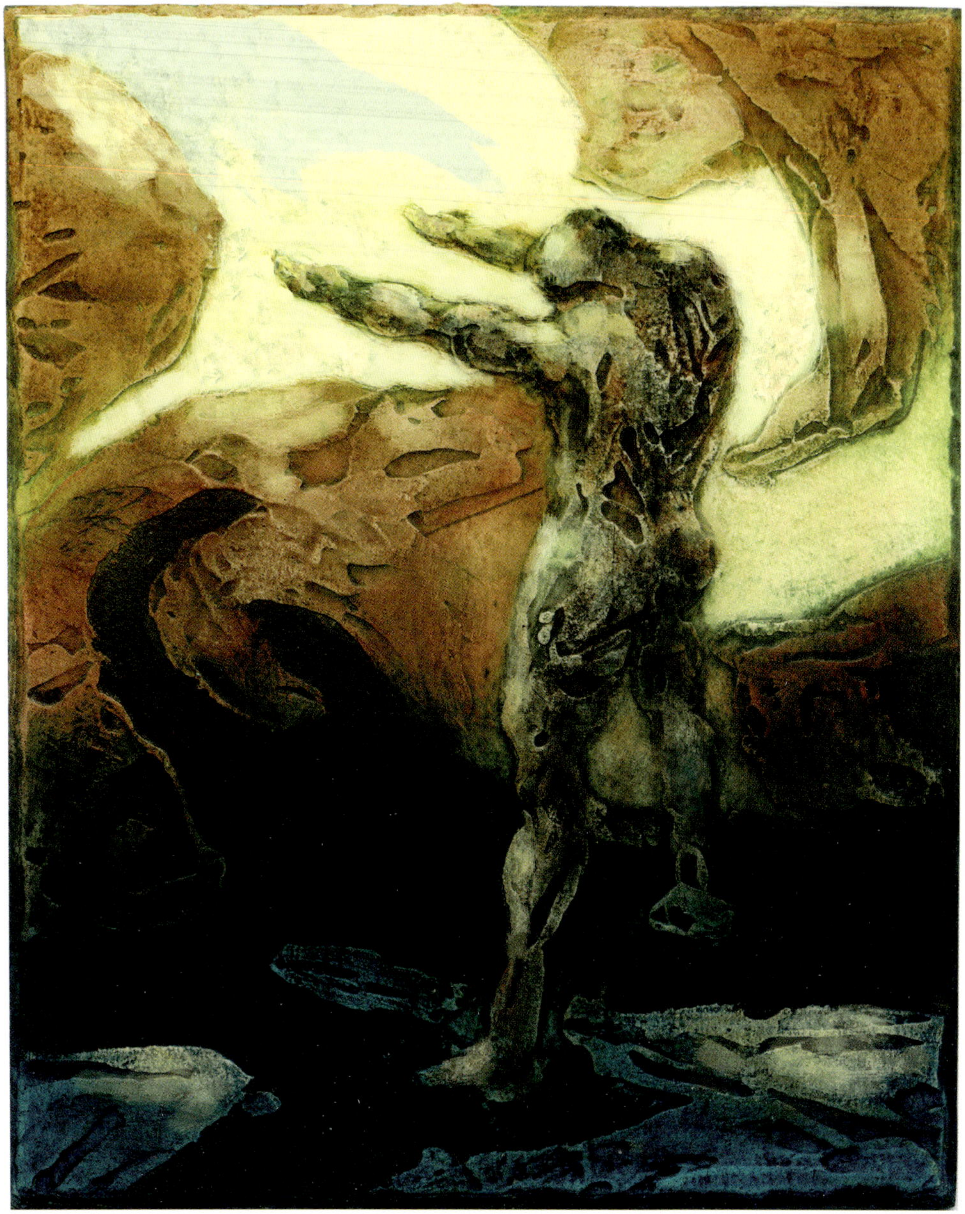

14

'We have the possibility of a great new culture, a world culture, a culture of the naked god found everywhere, accessible to all men if they choose'

Cecil Collins: Art and Modern Man

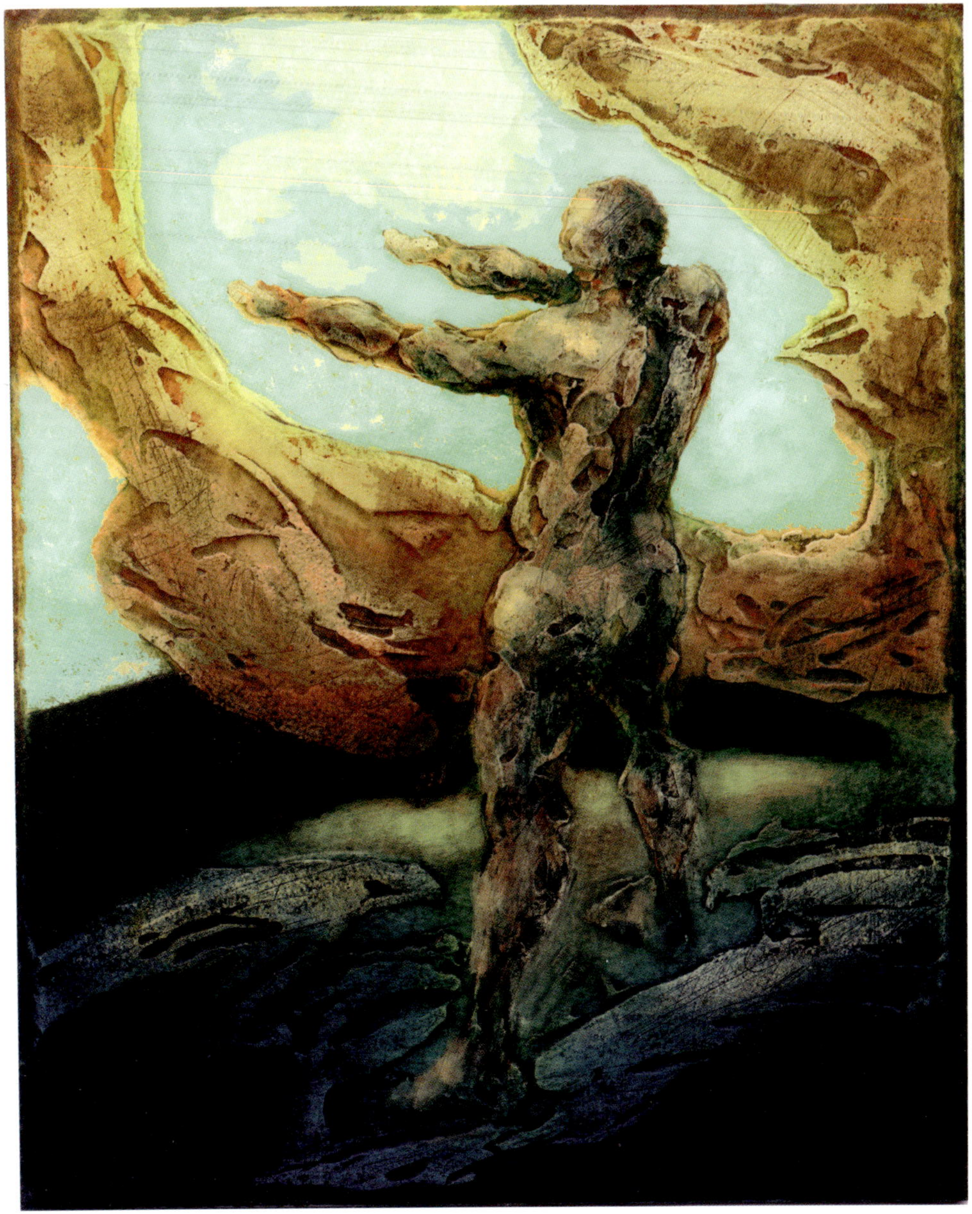

15

'We are beings before we are men and women, and it is from being that all art and poetry spring, and not from man or woman. The being within us contains the covenant that we made with God before the world began'

Cecil Collins: Hymn to Life

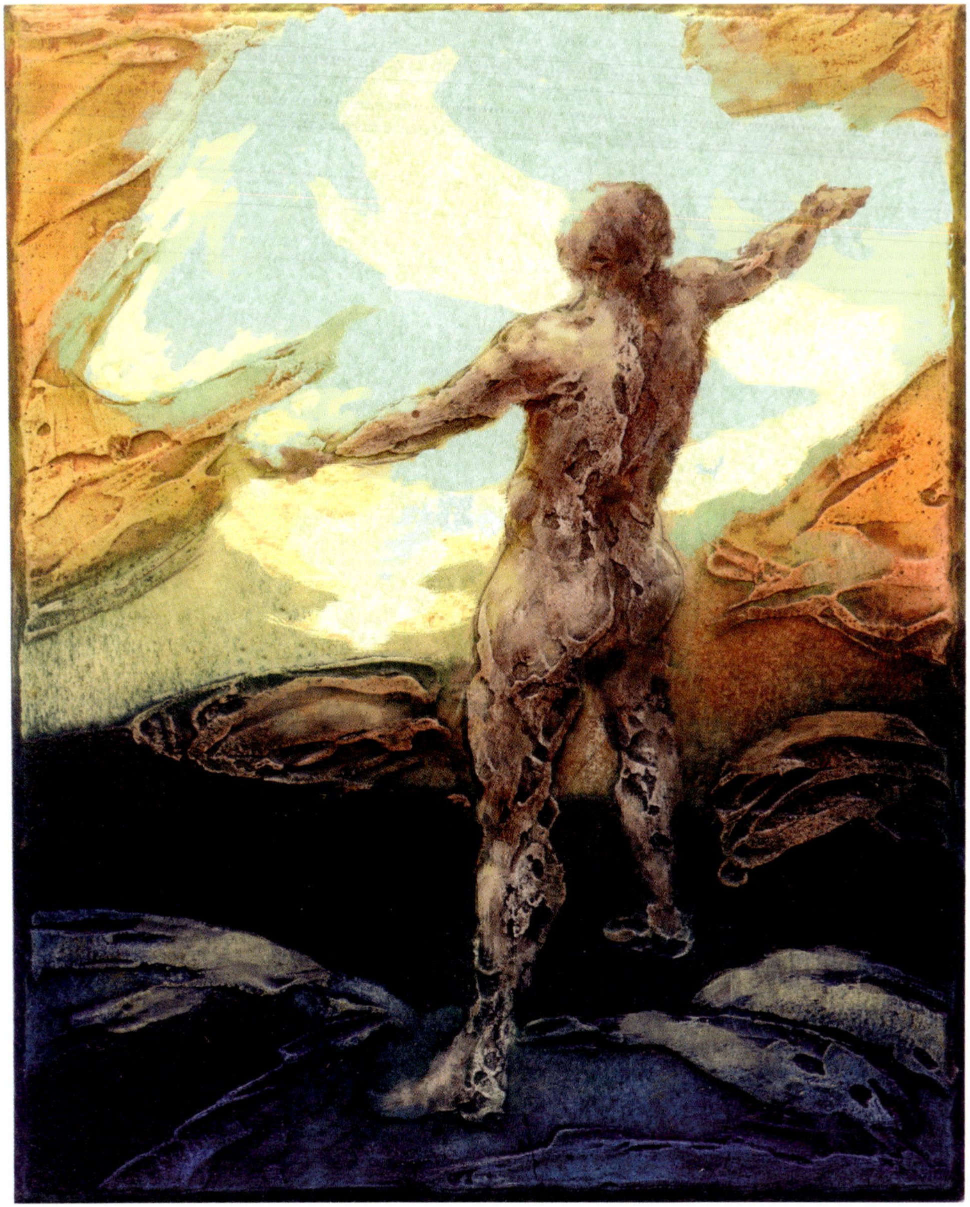

16

'The weariness of the body sends the soul upwards to open the leaves of the stars and read the secret poems written within them'

Cecil Collins: Meditations, book 2

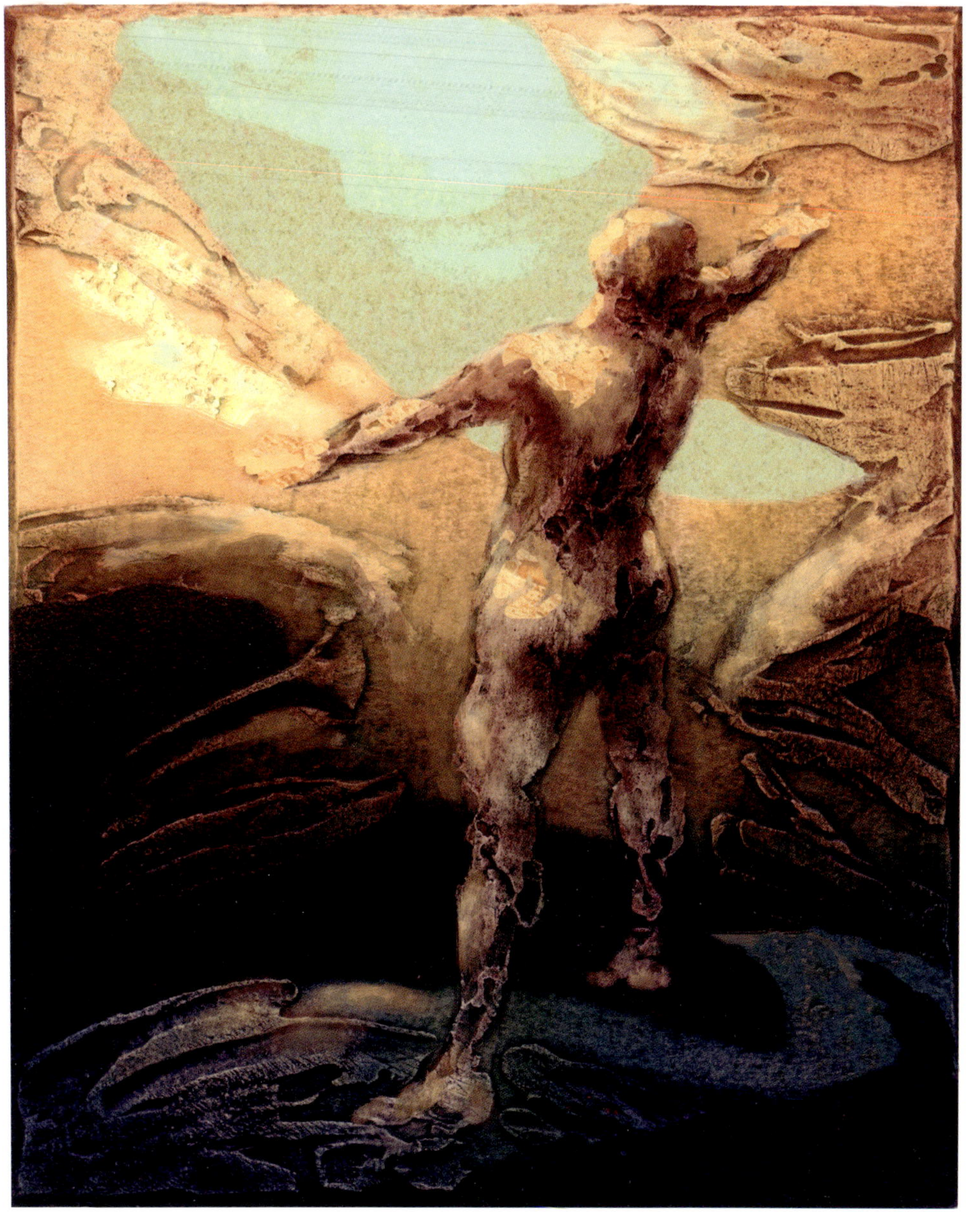

CECIL COLLINS: BIOGRAPHICAL NOTES

Cecil Collins was born in 1908 in Plymouth, Devon.

His talents were recognised and encouraged by his mother, who was herself an amateur artist, and in 1924 at the age of sixteen he was enrolled at Plymouth Art College. After three years at Plymouth he won a scholarship to continue his studies at the Royal College of Art in London, where he later won a prize for life drawing.

In 1931 he married Elizabeth, a fellow student who had been studying under the young sculptor Henry Moore. Elizabeth was to become a very devoted and supportive wife throughout Cecil's career, up to his death in 1989.

Cecil developed his work in the early thirties and became acquainted with other artists and poets whose work had a religious or spiritual theme, amongst whom were Eric Gill, David Jones and the American artist Mark Tobey.

Tobey had travelled in China and had become interested in Chinese calligraphy and painting techniques, and his influence shows in Cecil's calligraphic approach to drawing and painting.

In 1936 Cecil went to join Tobey at the artists' colony at Dartington in Devon, where they collaborated on their development of techniques. Cecil was later to take up a teaching post at Dartington.

Among the contemporary painters who were working at this time were Chagall, Ernst, Klee, Arp, Picasso and de Chirico, with whom Cecil was no doubt familiar and it is possible to see the influence of all of these painters in his work.

For a period he became associated with the Surrealist movement and had some of his work shown in the International Exhibition of 1936. However this affair was not to last as the materialistic doctrine of the Surrealists was incompatible with Cecil's basically spiritual approach.

At Dartington, as well as developing his painting and drawing, he wrote poetry and essays and met many figures from the literary and theatrical world who were also attracted there.

Cecil had been interested in the historical tradition of 'the Fool' since his youth, but it was not until he saw a drawing of a fool done by his wife in 1939 that he was inspired to develop the concept that had long lain dormant in his mind. The Fool represented for Cecil purity of consciousness and the human qualities of innocence and vulnerability, and together with 'the Angel' was to recur constantly throughout his subsequent work. In 1942 he began to write his best known essay 'The Vision of the Fool', which was published in 1947.

He left Dartington in 1943 and lived for several years in various locations in England until finally settling in Cambridge in 1948. He was now more widely known and was being shown with established London galleries on a regular basis. The postwar years were a period of intense activity and growing recognition. In 1949 he gained a commission for a design for the Edinburgh Tapestry Company, and in the same year had a painting accepted by the Tate Gallery.

In 1951 he was offered and accepted a part-time teaching post at the Central School of Art in London.

The following years were quite successful for Cecil; in 1958 he won a prize at the first John Moores exhibition in Liverpool and in 1959 had a retrospective exhibition at the Whitechapel Art Gallery.

Cecil had always experimented with different materials and techniques and in 1957 in his search for a freer expression, discovered what he called the 'matrix' technique. This was a more direct, spontaneous method of working which he later incorporated into his teaching methods in the life drawing classes.

Although his beliefs encompassed all faiths, he was awarded some interesting religious commissions: by the Oxford University Press in 1968 to make illustrations for the Oxford Illustrated Old Testament; by Chichester Cathedral for an altarpiece for the St. Clement Chapel in 1973 and a design for a stained glass window for St. Michael's Church, Basingstoke, in 1985.

In addition to his classes at the Central School, from 1972 he started to teach life drawing at the City Literary Institute in London, and this continued until 1987.

In 1975, at the age of 66, he was asked to retire from the Central School as he was beyond the usual retirement age. However due to vociferous protest from his students and several leading contemporary artists, the school backed down and he was reinstated. This confrontational situation also arose later at the 'City Lit' but the attempts each year to force him to retire were always defeated by his students.* Cecil nevertheless persevered through this period to produce some of his best work.

In 1979 he was awarded an MBE in recognition for his contribution to art, and in 1981 had a print retrospective exhibition at the Tate Gallery.

He was able to attend a further retrospective exhibition at the Tate just prior to his death in June 1989.

* For more detail refer to 'The Quest for the Great Happiness' pages 106 & 107.

THE LIFE DRAWING CLASSES

It was whilst attending another evening course at the City Literary Institute in London that I came to hear of Cecil Collin's life drawing classes. I had already done a certain amount of life drawing at Art School and also at the John Cass Art College with John Epstein, who was a hard and demanding teacher, but nothing was quite like Cecil's class. For three hours once a week one was transported to a different world.

My first impression of him was of a rather diffident and un-prepossessing man whose manner belied the authority he commanded over a class of perhaps fifteen to twenty mature students, who were professional or semi-professional artists and teachers or simply those interested in Cecil's particular approach to art.

When I began the classes in 1979, one still had a reasonable chance of getting on the course but by 1985 it had become so popular with the students that one had to queue all night during the enrolment week. The students themselves were the proof of his worth as a teacher. Amongst them he became in the end almost a cult figure.

So what was the essence of this special Cecil Collins teaching?

The nearest I can get to describing it is to say that he was able to show the artist how to 'abandon control' through the process of life drawing. This of course sounds absurd if not impossible, but when one has experienced it, it is less so. We spend our lives striving to gain control, to avoid letting affairs get out of control. The idea of abandoning control would appear to be the height of folly; but the 'Fool' was one of Cecil's most significant icons. When we have surrendered control we are vulnerable, at the mercy of others, in danger, our only resource is our basic intuition. Control operates through the intellect which has to be prevented from dominating for good art to result. This I believe was the main point of Cecil's teaching.

For the artist, allowing the intellect to dominate produces dead art. To give life to art it is necessary to by-pass the intellect and allow the expression of emotional spontaneity to operate. This idea is of course nothing new. For generations art teachers and critics have enjoined artists and students to 'loosen up', to 'express themselves', to 'be spontaneous', but few of them know how to bring it about. Cecil knew! His great achievement was in being able to draw out of his students the ability to freely express themselves through the vehicle of life drawing. This is why he was a great teacher, and his students recognised that fact.

Cecil had a long experience of the art world both as a practitioner and a teacher and he had arrived at a particular teaching method which was paradoxically very controlled and very structured. He was a strict disciplinarian and there was no question in his class of students 'doing their own thing'. On one occasion he said:

> *'There is no such thing as free expression. Freedom comes from an understanding of limitations'*

The students were asked to do some extraordinary things and those who were not able to accept them did not stay the course. The best way perhaps to explain Cecil's technique is simply to describe the progress of a typical class:

At the 'City Lit.' these took place in the afternoon and lasted for three hours. The model was in the centre of the room and the students sat along three sides at long trestle tables. The room was well lit from large windows on two sides. Cecil would not tolerate any artificial lighting, and so in the winter evenings we were often drawing in semi-darkness. One did the drawings on cheap cartridge paper or newsprint, normally at quite a fast pace. The drawings were done in black or sepia using Chinese stick ink or diluted gouache. One was expected to have seven small pots of varying tones ranging from black to the lightest grey. The basic implements comprised a range of Chinese brushes, reed pens, a quill pen, soft pencils, charcoal and red and black conté crayons.

The session began in the customary way with short poses, but even the longest pose was rarely more than five minutes. From the outset Cecil imposed his control. He would dictate precisely which tone of ink and which implement to use in which hand, for one was expected to use both hands together.

After a certain time, sometimes no more than seconds, he would say 'change', the model would alter the pose and the students would lay down another sheet of paper and start another drawing according to his instructions, one of which was to look only at the model, rather than the drawing. Drawing was initially done at great speed and the turnover was rapid.

'At the fast speed the analytical mind cannot work'

Some time later he would introduce music, played prior to each pose, and the students and the model would be asked to stand and move in response in whatever manner they felt appropriate. Such movements were naturally limited to the upper body and arms due to the limitations of space but within that constraint there was surprising scope for improvisation. At a certain moment Cecil would say 'stop' at which point the model would freeze and the students would sit down and draw according to the new instructions.

On occasions these instructions required one to draw with one's fingers, fist, heel of the hand, elbows, even the chin and the nose. Sometimes one was obliged to hold the instrument in the mouth (in which case three instruments were being used concurrently), or to place the paper on the floor and draw holding the instrument between the toes. His secret weapon was a bundle of three foot long brushes which he would distribute once the students were sufficiently 'softened up'. One had to balance one end on the shoulder and make the best of it with the other.

After two hours of suffering these indignities one was ready either to walk out or surrender. This was the critical moment. The overcoming of one's resistance, perhaps to being a 'fool'? By this time most new students would probably be feeling quite bewildered, if not confused; but Cecil knew what was happening. Art was happening! In the last hour there was a tangible atmosphere of calm intensity, the pace usually slowed down and some very good drawings were done; and that is all that matters in art, the end result, not the process of getting there or the 'suffering' of the artist.

Cecil understood that in the act of overcoming adversity, in this case one's resistance, a certain aesthetic power is revealed. It may even be a condition for such revelation, but that is speculation.

'The manifestation of beauty is often accompanied by pain'

Following Cecil's technique was in some strange way quite painful but the results made it worthwhile. At the end of the session one felt on the one hand emotionally exhausted and on the other exhilarated. For a brief period one had been transformed into an instrument of creativity through art, in contact with something fundamental within oneself, which enabled the release of a purity of line and form unsullied by the intellect. (I use the word 'intellect' here simply to refer to those processes that operate in the mind as opposed to those that operate in the emotions or feelings).

Cecil was not engaged in some sort of crusade against the intellect. He was merely trying to point out the dangers of over reliance on it especially in the realm of art. He equated the intellect with the masculine, which he saw as too dominant not only in art but in all walks of life. He believed in redressing the balance towards the intuitive, emotional, feminine faculty that lies within all of us, as though this were closer to our essential being. In this sense he was a real 'feminist'. However he maintained a sense of balance. I recollect on one of the rare occasions when he looked at the students' drawings he commented that he found the work 'too feminine'. Presumably by this he meant too vague, too indefinite, perhaps lacking in structure and boldness of line.

Although he denied it in his writings he was himself a considerable intellectual. His elaborate and detailed colour theory demonstrates this, and of course his highly structured teaching procedure could only be the result of very careful synthesis, a product of the mind.

All these aspects of Cecil's approach aroused my curiosity at the time. I had for some years studied with a particular esoteric school of philosophy whose practices were based on the teachings of Gurdjieff and Ouspensky and I was struck by the similarity with many of Cecil's ideas. At an opportune moment I questioned him about this and he revealed that he had indeed studied with the same group, but many years earlier. Gurdjieff was very interested in Sufism and oriental mysticism and had arrived at certain disciplines designed to 'wake people up', not least of which was his use of music and body movements, to bring them into the present and free them from their enslavement by the mind; not unlike the techniques employed in Zen Buddhism. I am sure that these influences had translated into Cecil's teaching.

There was no doubt that for the duration of the class one was obliged to be in the present, giving one's attention only to the drawing process and not to the endless thoughts in the mind. With the whole class equally concentrated a powerful atmosphere arose which was almost tangible. Anyone who has participated in group meditation or any similar co-operative experience will know of this particular form of energy.

In addition to the instructions about which instrument and which tone to use Cecil also made further distinctions about the parts of the instrument and how to hold it. (see page 51).

Throughout his teaching he laid stress on the masculine and feminine aspects of creativity and their interplay in the art of drawing and painting. This is probably best explained simply by reiterating verbatim the notes I made at the time, which are dated 15th October 1980 :

There are three canons of drawing:

1. Sensitivity
2. Rhythm
3. Vitality

Drawing is the language of response. Creativity is based on relationships – a marriage between the artist and object gives birth to the work of art, the drawing.

The drawing instruments

From hard to soft, masculine to feminine:

The Quill Pen	For very close fine work, short lines, incisive, precise, Intellectual, masculine, resistant.
The Reed Pen	Softer contact point, softer lines, varying density, longer strokes, Resistant.
The Brush	Very soft, delicate, fine or broad strokes, long bold lines or short marks, Feminine, pliant, submissive.
The Pencil	Provides the transition between the hard pen and the soft brush, Versatile, androgynous, hard and sharp or blunt and soft.

WAYS OF HOLDING THE INSTRUMENT

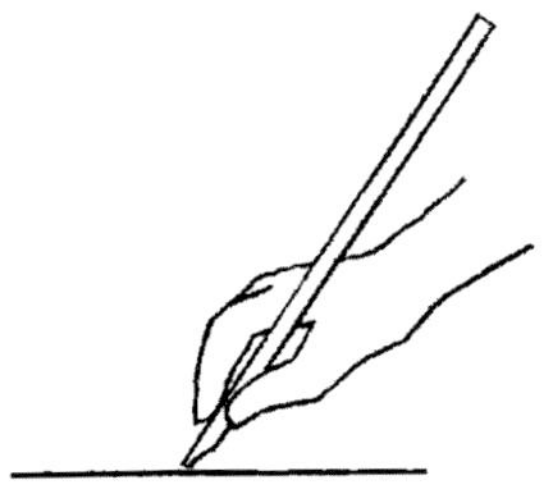

1. Very close – for precise work

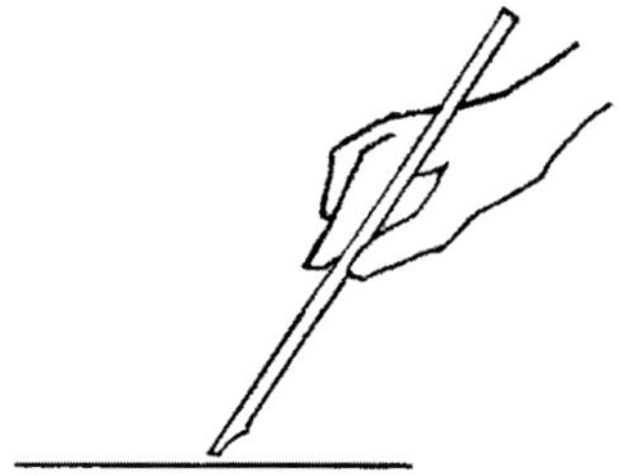

2. Held in the middle – for looser freer work

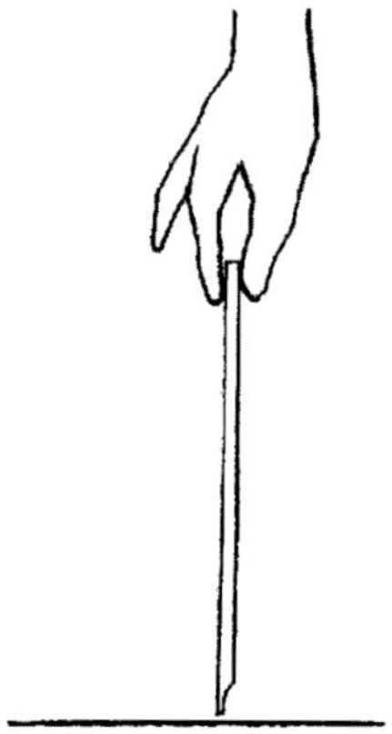

3. Held at the end – allowed to dangle

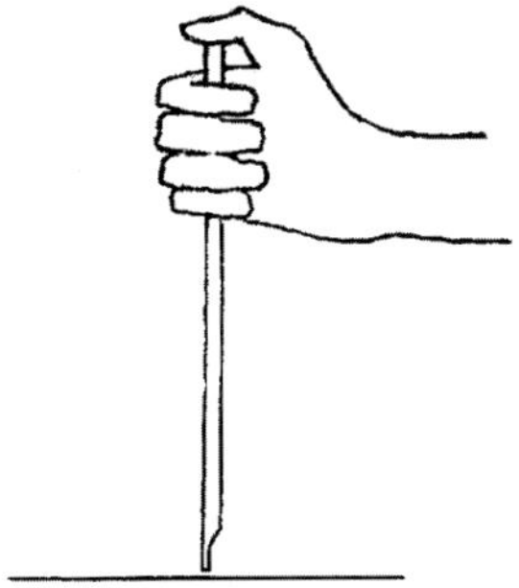

4. Held like a dagger

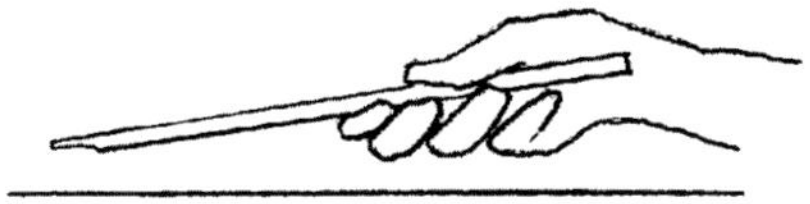

5. Held like a sword

The Brush

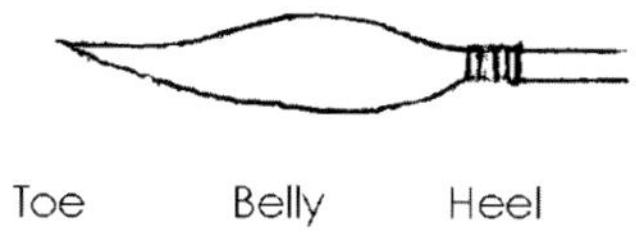

Ink tones

Seven tones of ink should be employed, using Chinese stick ink or black gouache diluted down to a very light tone with water only. Black is 1, middle tone is 4, lightest is 7.

Every person must know his own field of energy. The field is guarded by cortesia (or courtesy) – for example by bowing and respecting the space around forms or people.

GENERAL COMMENTS

Over the years attending the life classes, Including his colour life painting classes during the summer period, I took notes of the various statements that Cecil made which struck a chord in me. I repeat them here without comment and in no particular order or context, but simply as a collection representing Cecil's views at the time:

'Creativity is a sense of wonder'

'All creativity is to do with clarity not muddle'

'One purpose of drawing is to take the insight of fast speeds and feed them back to the slow speeds, although the slow speeds have their own insights'

'The expression of light is through tone'

'One cannot teach anyone how to paint, one can only introduce someone to techniques'

'There is no such thing as a painting – only a study'

'Be as sceptical as you can, the only thing scepticism can't stand up to is the truth'

'Art can serve God or the Devil equally' – Quoting Dostoevsky ?

'Art is the battleground where God and the Devil struggle for the soul of Man' – Quoting Dostoevsky?

'Man's natural home is Paradise'

'Finally there are only two basic questions:
Who am I ? What am I living for ?

Cecil also conducted another ceremony representing an acknowledgment of the instruments and materials. This took place in the half-light of dusk and I recollect that each student sat behind a lighted candle and was required to kiss each instrument and the paper, a sort of sacrament. It was done with great solemnity and was indeed another moving experience which seemed entirely appropriate at the time.

On the occasion of the postures ceremony Cecil gave a general talk which I noted down as well as I was able, and to end this account I propose simply to reiterate again the notes I made at the time, which are dated 8th October 1980:

> *Society at present is dominated by the masculine element. The masculine characteristics are cerebral, thinking, analytic, rational. This is reflected in the surrounding contemporary architecture which is hard, rational, uncompromising, undecorated. The masculine element is therefore descriptive. Academic art is relentlessly descriptive but it lacks the element which true art seeks. Great art is about a form of reality which is indescribable but nevertheless we can recognise it when we see it.*
>
> *The artist is always seeking the invisible, the formless, the un-definable. He must be prepared to make mistakes, to make a fool of himself. He must strive to forget himself, his own self-image, self considering. Only then will the true forms emerge from his being. This is the act of creativity.*
>
> *We are unable to let the life force flow from us because we have encased it with habit and self-considering. It is possible to break through this crust and release the true energy within all of us. We have to learn to be conscious and alert and to concentrate our attention. All great art demonstrates these qualities.*

BIBLIOGRAPHY

William Anderson — *Cecil Collins: The Quest for the Great Happiness*
Barrie and Jenkins, London 1998

Cecil Collins — *The Vision of the Fool and other Writings*
Compiled and edited by Brian Keeble
Golganooza Press, Ipswich 1994

Cecil Collins — *Meditations, Poems and Pages from a Sketchbook*
Compiled and edited by Brian Keeble
Golgonooza Press, Ipswich 1997

Judith Collins — *Cecil Collins: A Retrospective Exhibition*
The Tate Gallery, London 1989

Cecil Collins — *Angels*
Compiled and edited by Stella Astor
Fools' Press, London 2004

ACKNOWLEDGEMENTS

For their help and advice my thanks are due to:
Stella Astor, Lesley Crick, Ruth Eisenhart, Jim Felici, John Hawkins, Ken and Juliet Jones, Brian Keeble, Neville Rolt and Tony Wills.

Quotations from Cecil Collins' essays are reproduced by kind permission of the Tate Gallery Archives.